W9-CBS-591

Fisher-Price®

®

Little People®

Opposite Safari

Modern Publishing
A Division of Unisystems, Inc.
New York, New York 10022
Series UPC Number: 19615

Let's go on safari.
There's nothing to lose.
Remember your camera,
And wear comfy shoes.

We're hunting for opposites.
Search **high** and **low**.
The jungle is full of them.
Here we go!

A lion stays **dry** in the hot jungle sun.

A hippo thinks being all **wet** is more fun.

A **fat** elephant takes a bath by the pool.
A **skinny** snake slithers in shade to stay cool.

A colorful parrot is **loud** when he talks.
A black and white zebra takes nice **quiet** walks.

To the **left** of the watering hole there's a tree.
To the **right** there's a leopard who's staring at me.

A monkey has lunch **right-side up** on a limb.
His brother hangs **upside-down**, grinning at him.

A **tall** giraffe can reach up high.
A turtle's so **short**, he doesn't try.

A **big** lion roars and shows her claws.
Her **little** one's safe in her strong paws.

A parrot flies **over** the nest he has made.
A rhino stands **under** the tree,
in the shade.

A crocodile lurks **in** a cool hollow log.
His friend, who stays **out**, is a little green frog.

Some coconuts hang **on** a tree in a bunch.
One falls **off**. We'll have it for lunch.

The monkeys climb **up**, the lions lie **down**,
The elephants **smile**, the rhinos **frown**.

The **day** is gone, the shadows creep,
And **night** is here. It's time to sleep.